About the Author

Milagros Passeron was born in Buenos Aires, Argentina. She is a poet and writer.

Marks of a Body

Milagros Passeron

Marks of a Body

Olympia Publishers
London

www.olympiapublishers.com
OLYMPIA PAPERBACK EDITION

Copyright © Milagros Passeron 2024

The right of Milagros Passeron to be identified as author of this work has been asserted in accordance with sections 77 and 78 of the Copyright, Designs and Patents Act 1988.

All Rights Reserved

No reproduction, copy or transmission of this publication may be made without written permission.
No paragraph of this publication may be reproduced, copied or transmitted save with the written permission of the publisher, or in accordance with the provisions of the Copyright Act 1956 (as amended).

Any person who commits any unauthorised act in relation to this publication may be liable to criminal prosecution and civil claims for damage.

A CIP catalogue record for this title is available from the British Library.

ISBN: 978-1-80439-902-6

This is a work of fiction.
Names, characters, places, and incidents originate from the writer's imagination. Any resemblance to actual persons, living or dead, is purely coincidental.

First Published in 2024

Olympia Publishers
Tallis House
2 Tallis Street
London
EC4Y 0AB

Printed in Great Britain

Dedication

To my sister and brother.

Acknowledgements

Thank you to my friends and my parents for being a huge support as I wrote these poems.

Baking

From beneath someone's waist
I wait, shoelaces untied,
and backpack in my hand.
She takes something white,
to sprinkle on the bridge
of my nose,
and I catch the scent
of sugar and dough.

Maybe I spoke to say
what I saw,
or maybe she knew
it wasn't all.
That the work I couldn't
yet see,
would be the most fun for me.

Sitting on cold marble stone,
hands sticking
to sugary dough,
watching from above.
I feel the shoelaces
swing back and forth,
because my feet are now,
far from the floor.

In that scale I got,
a little fear to fall,
but she cooked next to me,
kneading, mixing,
standing tall.

The dog barks
and my talking never stops.
A high-pitched voice
tells me her show is on.
But she stays and answers,
laughing in between.
Maybe I asked something odd,
yet she still answered,
opening the oven door.

Grandma

Cigarettes, wine,
Sugar and spice,
And the taint of vice,
My laugh stands unaccompanied
In her home,
But only today, standing alone.

Buried behind the far-left wall,
All our laughs are stored,
For her to dust
In tactless talks,
Made for the moments
We've enjoyed the most.

After all is accounted for,
She's sugar and spice,
And just a little bit of vice,

Daughter's Patrimony

Whose eyes stare back at me?
Whose manners I see then,
His or mine?
I'll plead for love but refuse his praise,
How from a young age,
All I've done is emulate,
His way of feeling all the way,
Getting anxious everywhere,
To now condemn this, in him and me.

He's made me in his reflection,
Heritage of fantasy reading,
Fun sweet music and,
A patrimony in movie taste,
And all he'll say now is,
How little he's made of himself.

He's admired the way,
My arms seem to stretch out,
Reach for every passion project I can realise,
But I never come round to our house,
Just pick up the mistakes,
I've dropped in front of him,
Like carpet stains and incomplete plates,
Asking for clemency.

You've wasted your time,
Poured the purest love,
You could find inside yourself,
On a daughter you dreamt,
Well, now I've turn out like that,
Rekindling the crooked corners,
Of your mind.

You've tried ever so hard to hide,
A cracked cast,
Made from the best you could conjure up,

Well, at least you tried,
You're not God,
And I'm not a miracle.

You're just a father,
And I'm my father's daughter,
Lurking outside the room,
Waiting,
To become him.

Mother

Have you seen?
May's bush this spring,
packed white speckles,
that almost resemble a fairy's dream,
a cotton glaze,
soft as clouds,
dressed in green gowns.

In Spanish, *corona de novia,*
the name I heard,
translated 'bride's crown',
maybe it's referred to,
by that name in English too,
I don't really know,
but I remember them first,
from pictures of my mom,
on her wedding day.

It was her Spring,
In the *Cinderella* dress,
I kid you not,
my sister and I used to laugh,
about how perfect that was,
a crown of those flowers.

And a bouquet of them in mom's hand,
my dad a prince in stature and poise,
by her side,
a princess of twenty-three,
with a couple of degrees under her sleeve.

On her way to be a queen,
of the house she dreamed,
not without imperfections,
she is human after all,
though I swear those pictures,
almost make you forget.

She leans on the perfectionist side,
and rushes to get things done,
often saying "how much better something would be,
if you would just let me help you with it."

But that's about it.
A mother with *Cinderella's* charm,
a teacher of kindness and strength.
She's a May's bush through and through,
Question remains,
how her sprouts became,
low summer grains?

This spring I remember her smile,
when I told her how much I loved,
those white flowers with green gowns.
I remember how the things I inherited,

are not in my body,
but in my curious love for trinkets so old,
you can almost feel time on them,
in my love for food and celebrating,
or the softness that makes me cry quite often.

Maybe my Spring won't be,
in *Cinderella's* dress,
maybe it'll be just me and a pen,
and blossoming to summer's grains.

But if I could at least have one May's bush in my hand,
and catch some traces of mom in myself,
that is a haunting resembling beauty.

A Sister Kind of Love

Whenever I need,
To ground myself again,
I think of my sister,
Surrounding me,
Her voice ringing,
Through our years,
Where right over me,
She loomed, protected.

She knows,
follows what she wants,
Never mind causing trouble,
She loves that,
In the uncertainty she lives in,
There's assurance to find.

She steps in way too much,
wants to talk all the time,
She's everything I'll ever want to be,
Idiosyncrasies and all.

Now she lives elsewhere,
And I've just found,
All the things in her,
That drive me mad,

Are just bits of me,
We've been trading.

Over the years,
Passed down ornaments,
Echoing off each other,
When we've run out of things to say.

She knows where my wounds are made,
Whether to place her hand over them,
Or dig through the scabs.

She's there, watching over me,
That's what sisters are for,
And I hope she knows,
I'd never wish for anything else.

Little Brother

There's a rhythm to his day,
The words scribbled across the room,
Planning out the way,
The exercising and practicing,
The perfecting and organizing,
Hard to picture him as irritating,
As a big sister would find him.

Pulling at a strand of hair,
Or shouting from the other side of the room,
An insult smart and perfected,
With the tick of the clock.

There we find it,
The ability to craft something,
Through the days and the years,
To be effortlessly good at everything.

It's hard to admit that I envy it,
With his liberty of boyhood,
Unconcerned for what it means,
To lose yourself trying to be a nice girl,
His capacity to feel things lightly,
Excuse himself from conflict,
And give scarce comfort and hugs,

In the perfect timing.

I suppose my little chaos is charming,
And I've learnt to like it a bit,
I'm still working through,
on controlling it.

But my little brother,
Though exasperating and,
full of himself by moments,
I think I envy the most,
How proud we all are,
Of how better you've become,
At silently loving.

Summer's Type of Time

There's another set of time,
Reserved for the summer house.

A morning that sticks like slime,
Fizzy and wearing undefined lines,
To fit with every one of our routines,
For waking up.

The first round with grandparents,
Sipping tea and news,
Sometimes interrupted by us,
Going to the occasional overnight hike.

But most days their silence goes on,
For an hour or so,
Till the second round comes:
My cousin eager to get to the lake,
Our moms enjoying the first light of day.

Then comes the rest,
(Most of us at least)
Swallowing cereal, coffee,
Or chocolate milk,
Munching toast with jam,
Butter or cheese.

It's funny to see,
After an hour goes by,
Grandpa walking with his hat,
Sweater and cane,
In 40°c,
Never breaking a sweat.

While all of us, save a teenager still asleep,
Go to change into our swimsuits,
And light-washed jeans.

By noon the teen of that given year,
Has woken up already,
And gone down to the beach,
Where all of us let Time know,
It can change,
For the afternoon show,
This Time is slow yet on beat,
Giving us the space to:
Play and eat, shout and swim.

To read and drink a bit of tea,
Take a nap or walk with the trees,
Maybe pick some raspberries.

Talk with some friends,
And eat dinner very late,
'Cause it's still light outside,
We don't want Time to go to waste',
Then night comes and Time,
Turns to slime again.

We look at each other,
Painted after a day in the sun:
His freckles pop up,
And her hair's a lighter shade,
To match with the way, he smiles,
After playing for hours with us.

Grandma says goodnight,
Though she'll stay up and write,
Then we ask our moms for a bit more Time,
To enjoy the same movie,
We watch every single night.

Dads say 'let them stay late',
While they walk slowly,
To each of their beds,
Moms kiss us goodnight,
And go for a well-deserved rest.

Then it's us,
Reluctantly admitting defeat,
To our closing eyelids,
But the teen stays up,
For a little while.

Goes out with friends,
And drinks a bit,
The type of fun,
We'll all have, sometimes.

Finally, they walk back,

On tiptoes after midnight,
Flop down on the bed,
And sleep, Time changes again.

Paint It without You

I'd paint a life without stairs,
Without climbing high,
Paint it without wild travels,
Strangers and landscapes fondly tucked in my mind.

Without bits and pieces,
Of the course of my life,
When I was with people,
I'll never love.

Without butterflies,
Without a moon,
But never in a million years,
Could I paint a life without you.

It wouldn't be mine,
Without your hug,
Your voice,
Without your unexpected call.

All the little parts of you,
I value so much more,
Then any wild night,
I could find.

So, please linger,
Please value your heart,
Strive higher,
Build skyscrapers,
Out of dreams,
Being witness to that,
Is all the joy I ever want?

First Crush

Childhood builds drawings,
Pictures in unsteady lines,
That trace lunchtime talks,
then turns to,
Our first finish line.

Paths open wide for us,
Morph to codes in exchange,
Practically made for the limited,
Time our paths cross for,
Often but short,
Traces of lines.

No wonder,
I want my drawings marked,
The various codes,
That have taken on depth,
Engraved on me,
Turning me into,
A beautiful scrapbook,
Of memories.

Teacup Smell

The whole world smelled like sleep,
Like the worn teacup that haunts your dreams,
I walked out and smelled,
The whole world in the porcelain,
Thick veins of bright dust,
Stirring violin's strings around,
The whole teacup held in my hand,
As I stepped out into the
Haunted dream,
Held the whole world
of stirred dust,
With teacup smell.

First One Gone

Curious how death arrives
Not at your door, but
slithering about
how it says hello.
Catching the crystal-eyed soul,
without warning, in a snatch, like snow,
Blowing her rose coloured laugh,
Across paperback,
into the furthest classroom,
we'll ever share.

She dusts our joy with death's hello,
With an introduction,
and invitation,
For the unshakable hearts,
to fall.

Florence Welch

Florence Welch, have you heard of her?
The songs turned hymns of humanity and love,
Otherworldly in her voice,
Everyone a tear of the heart,
Vices and virtues,
Of human nature,
Dug in intimate breaths,
Of her years lived,
The depths of despair tied,
Around the grossly mundane,
I wish to reach her strength,
Shown in the demolishing of herself,
To rebuild her own heart again,
I wish I can read,
Every verse I write,
As urgently,
I wish I can compel,
A room half as much,
Make them float,
Into the stars I love,
And see what's earth,
Got to give to us now.

Drunkenness

When we came to,
And found the washed-up songs,
Secrets and loving looks,
That were blasted far too loud.

We found the strangers of,
Drunkenness falling from the night,
Fizzing as the sun comes up.

The strangers whose screams,
Sound too far now for anyone to catch,
To take back.

In innocence and uninhibited looks,
Strangers loved,
Slowly, surely,
in intervals of shouts.

Blushing Blooms

Blushed bodies and,
Wrapped arms,
Appear as untroubled,
Happy gasps,
Yet how can it be seen,
In the same light,
As fellow flowers,
Blooming by each other's side,
Understanding,
Of one another's lines.

Blushing blooms,
In early spring,
Fine flowers,
Might yet thrive,
Into the firsts,
Falls of snow.

Where I Fit

I fit in the trees,
In the weeping willows,
Beside mud, sand, and river rain,
Singing civil better than voices can,
In the larch leaves,
Next to mountains, songbirds, and snow,
Breathing deeper than the souls in my home,
In every tree top I dive,
Drowning in the beating stars,
That tattoo themselves onto trunks,
Like the creatures that leave their,
Individual scratch,
In the trees I reside,
Reading the letters, I'll never write.

Framed

I've lived in four rooms at least,
Big, small,
Or just enough to fit my things,
One with a window wall,
Another's window's barred,
One in a van,
Had a window the size of my hand,
A last one, exactly the size of my body.

In two rooms, blinds dropped,
Loudly every night,
Opposite rooms, had curtains,
That sang goodbye to the light.

All the ones I lived in,
All the ones that guarded my bed,
Had windows that never,
Closed all the way.

The clear thin glass, stuck in every place.
Fit perfectly in its throne,
But left one little edge,
A line at the bottom to let in the cold,
Never ceased in defeat,
Despite every loud effort.

To make it stop,
Every night I laid down in bed, my back to the glass,
Hoping tonight, I had closed it shut.

Then the weighing colour under my eyes,
And thousand little minions,
That never sleep and live,
In my mind,
Would shake me awake,
And tear up the bed.

So, every one of those nights I heard,
The thin pitched sound,
Coming from outside,
Softly brushing and wrapping around my arms.

My ears would feel sharper by every gust of wind,
My head a little lighter by,
Hearing the window sing.

So, I knew the window's edge,
Had cracked in every room,
Followed me everywhere,
Wherever I moved.

To bring a little reminder,
A little voice to say,
A day may be tougher than,
You can fit within yourself,
But a little edge of the world will wait,
For when you want to come out,
And play.

Sun Dance

I saw the sun dancing in my room,
Following the curtain's call,
and rhythm of the fan.

It speeds then breathes,
Silent in the morning cool,
I saw it excuse itself,
round bedroom shadows,
Glasses standing in ovation,
And the scent of half sleep,
That is left in my clothes,
I watched the sun dance around it all,
Greet the birds, the singing dew.

To Never Die

Open the door,
Crawl to my corner,
Where I lie, in conscious dreams,
Bring every giggle,
And the ugliest night,
Drop them all,
between the dark and my chest.

Stir till you linger,
Is stronger than wine,
Till the bruise on the bed,
That bent for you,
Can never dwindle,
till you have crossed my heart,
and hoped to never die.

Sisyphus' Fashion

Maybe I should flush,
And pray to whatever deity,
I can find,
That my heart shrinks away,
It seems wild,
To fall in love in days,
Like a breeze,
Then crash further,
Down with each final text.

Goodness hopes my heart,
Has enough life,
For when finality,
Doesn't come to pass,
When, at the tip of my toes,
Already waiting for.

The cracked ache I've lived,
With for so long,
No words seem to pull me down,
When I find that other heart,
That fits alongside mine.

Until then I wait,
in Sisyphus' fashion,

I go day after day,
Rolling my heart up.

For everyone to see and grab,
Scratch, stain,
Do with it as you please,
But in shameless despair,
I ask,
Take it.

Infatuation

Don't tell me if it's delusion,
Feed my idiocy abundantly,
With feasts of comfort songs,
Threaded out selectively,
A trail left for starvation.

To cherish, to crawl after,
Ignorant to how pride might ever feel,
Your eyes still smell like honey to me,
I don't want to be happy,
There's nothing left to say then.

The calmness of the sea,
has come to torment my sleep,
disowning the dream I should've been living,
instead I'm chasing ghosts,
Wrapping myself around nothing.

I suppose I've grown out,
And tore up the dress of contentment,
So here I dig my knees in sand,
Begging for repentance,
you're truly too kind of a man.

Fucking Say It

"I love you's"
Don't come easy to me,
Too strange,
To my mouth, my teeth,
If it's not a reply,
To another saying it.

But I hope "I love you's"
Shaped into cookies,
And dinners are enough,
The time in knowing,
The way to someone's,
Home by heart.

The hand that clings,
On your arm too much,
I've tried to write,
I love you'd in that,
Carve hearts in chocolate pieces,
Wrap it in a gift.

I'm trying,
To say it though,
I promise someday,
I will.

Not Love

Not in the way a finger traces my ear,
Or how the words fall over each other,
Not in the way my finger twists,
And wraps around my hair,
And how they get lost in it,
Not how their stories lose me.

In the middle of nothing,
Floating around,
Not in the way I'm certain, sure,
They'll lean in the remaining space,
And live an hour in my car.
Not in the love way.

Where my heart loops in itself,
Mulling, rewinding myself to the second,
Where the split of them and me,
Fell with their words,
Not in my loveless drive,
In the cold night.

Dog

On white cold floors,
Where silver and glasses quietly accompany,
The night falls into quarter to three,
The dog whines for a lighter air,
And I sit,
Beside the dog, in the heavy night,
Chilled by white floors under me.

As the clock ticks on the other room,
I sit, wondering about you,
The mix of wine and voicemail tone,
Run down my throat,
In rhythm with the sweat,
On the back of my neck,
On the side of my arm,
While the dog turns and stares,
At the fixed wooden door.

I sit, thanking no one's home,
A piece of me on our last spring call,
The height of summer is weighed upon me,
And he whines again,
The floor is no longer cold.

Child

I've daughters in gold,
Sons in kingdom crowns,
Enclosed,
I've children in moulds,
Kept for ages in these worlds
And seconds of open eyes.

I've warmed with fingers,
Held in place with palms,
To keep for a time to come,
A little soul to meet the,
World with open eyes,
Taking my hand.

Memories

Build me in memories,
Of a mother's hand,
A father's night-time tale,
The comfort to precious souls,
Their defines in,
The dark of the night,
Build me out of,
Uniforms I've worn,
disjointed of a heart,
I had yet to know,
Build me in friendships,
In snapping viciousness,
Of girlhood bleeding,
On the world.

Unknowingly to anyone,
With the eyes to turn away,
And hands to clasp,
In innocence,
Build me bathed in,
Baptism of restlessness,
And the water,
That would dare,
Wash it away,
Build me in reclaiming,

Kind lawlessness,
Born of my fellow,
Marble heart.

Who Is That?

Art and poets call in a plea,
For everyone to lay bare,
Shed the comfort of guarding,
Leave the bricks they've grown,
Ever so fond of,
Turn towards sincerity,

How wonderful truth can be.

Still, I fall one step behind,
Staying in the questioning,
Could I ever show you the exhibition of me,
Without knowing who that is?
Even if someone could find the way in,
All I could say is,
That way of smiling at the top,
Ripples from a great grandparent,
Down to the gestures and all.

I think, I have no picture of them,
The passions for all living things by the right,
Was passed by my greatest friend,
How she just fell in love with the world,
I've lost contact with her,
Oh, that bit by the centre,

The set good intentions,
An unromantic teacher helped me write them.

I wonder if he's changed,
Now this,
The cross by the end of the room,
We're trying to take it down,
But see, the wall's just so empty without it,
I put forth an exhibition,
In fragments that never stuck,
They fall and new ones come.

The heaviest though,
Has cemented itself on the wall,
Nothing as permanent.

As the haunting of faith,
I'll show you the exhibition,
Of whom I wish to be,
That one follows a thread,
Effortlessly,
Of single pieces stepping,
Onto the next,
Bold with colours,
And warmth to radiate.

I guess then,
I'd say the exhibition you see,
Is one of second-hand pieces,
And cracked with regret,
Never whole,

And no sense of self,
How could it?
Hand me downs,
Were always too big for me.

Purple Lips

Purple lips,
Purple whispers,
In 2000' stickers,
And your punk obsession,
Has been dying
On the strainer.

Our worldwide hope,
And month-old veggies,
Rotting quite resembling,
The tongues of boys,
We've been eating,
Night by night.

Rigorously as a,
Year goal work out,
And a girl to pine for,
Too smart and unattainable,
So here we've been dying,
With stickers our age.

Plastered by our sisters,
To entertain ourselves,
Uncomfortably young,
For us to conceptualise,

The blue burning,
Flames of a sad world,
I would drown in.

Learnt So Far

There are a pair of hands somewhere
Making sure vegetables grow
Carrots and apricots
Divided by handmade signs
All so a few days later
They smile, reach out their arm
And from the ripe fruit,
I take a bite
And someone met them before
Bought a head or lettuce or more
To make a home of faces and voices they know
A meal to sit down, eat and enjoy

Then I follow a street
To a garden I've never seen before
Try to admire the work inside a gallery
Of tapestries I don't know the story of
But hands and minds picked
Those threads, cut the length
Someone's body strained
To lay their existence
Weave it in between back stitches
On exposed fabric
Stared and stitched
A piece for warmth,

Art and power to be performed
So many hands, so many bodies
Rippling themselves beyond mortality
Evidence that someone took joy
On what they built
Sometimes my mind goes numb
Thinking of so much of everything
Draping over and over the world
Between the mess and madness
Of fires we've undeniably sparked
And fed,
We're still reaching, hoping
That there's a purpose after all
In enjoying a small dark plum
In staring at art we can't talk back to
In growing a thin delicate plant
That'll be gone in a day or two
Yet in each new rambling
And wrapping of my own
Thoughts around each other
The best I could find is nothing.
But that which in
The middle of cobbled streets
Drizzled my body in calm
Convincingly resembling
Tears and melancholy.
That in our desperation
To leave loud evidence,
And get remembrance
We find both the crumbling
Of everything

And sacred purpose

To be stupid in love
And talk to someone on the bus
To taste the food someone spent
Their scarce time preparing
To worry about the grains of sand
That are sad movies
And shiny pieces of art
To reach desperately our arms out
And find someone to hold on to
As we fall through.

Maybe Someday

Will I do it someday?

Eat well and sleep,
When I feel my body needs it?
And reply to people timely,
Orderly, practising reciprocity,
Will I care my teeth falling out,
From brushing them too roughly,
And the seams of my skin breaking,
As my nails carve towards something within it?
And will I stop searching in the dark for reasons to cry,
Will the need to cry habitually ever die?
More than tragic and sad,
It's become ridiculous now.

A performance for myself,
Of my own inability to cope
With the fact that I am breathing today,
That somehow, accidentally,
I've extended my existence out,
And now have bits of me in others,
As I have bits of them,
And I have a responsibility to nurture it.

But it is much more comforting,

To sink beneath covers and salt and water,
And maybe that's why I love the sea so much.

Because it is tears and their catalyst,
Amplified, connecting us.

Maybe I find it beautiful to swim,
In the vast sadness of saltwater and the beach.

Trying to make my body as lost as my head is,
Delivering ripples of my fingers on the sea,
An overture to the following wave.

And I let it crash over me,
Much more comforting,
Then caring correctly.